AF361203

Sex on a Budget: Love and Other Things I Can't Afford

Cali Loria

BookLeaf Publishing
India | USA | UK

Sex on a Budget: Love and Other Things I Can't Afford © 2022 Cali Loria

All rights reserved.

No part of this publication may be reproduced, stored in a retrieval system, or transmitted, in any form or by any means, electronic, mechanical, photocopying, recording or otherwise, without the prior written permission of the presenters.

Cali Loria asserts the moral right to be identified as author of this work.

Presentation by *BookLeaf Publishing*

Web: www.bookleafpub.com

E-mail: info@bookleafpub.com

ISBN: 9789357214483

First edition 2022

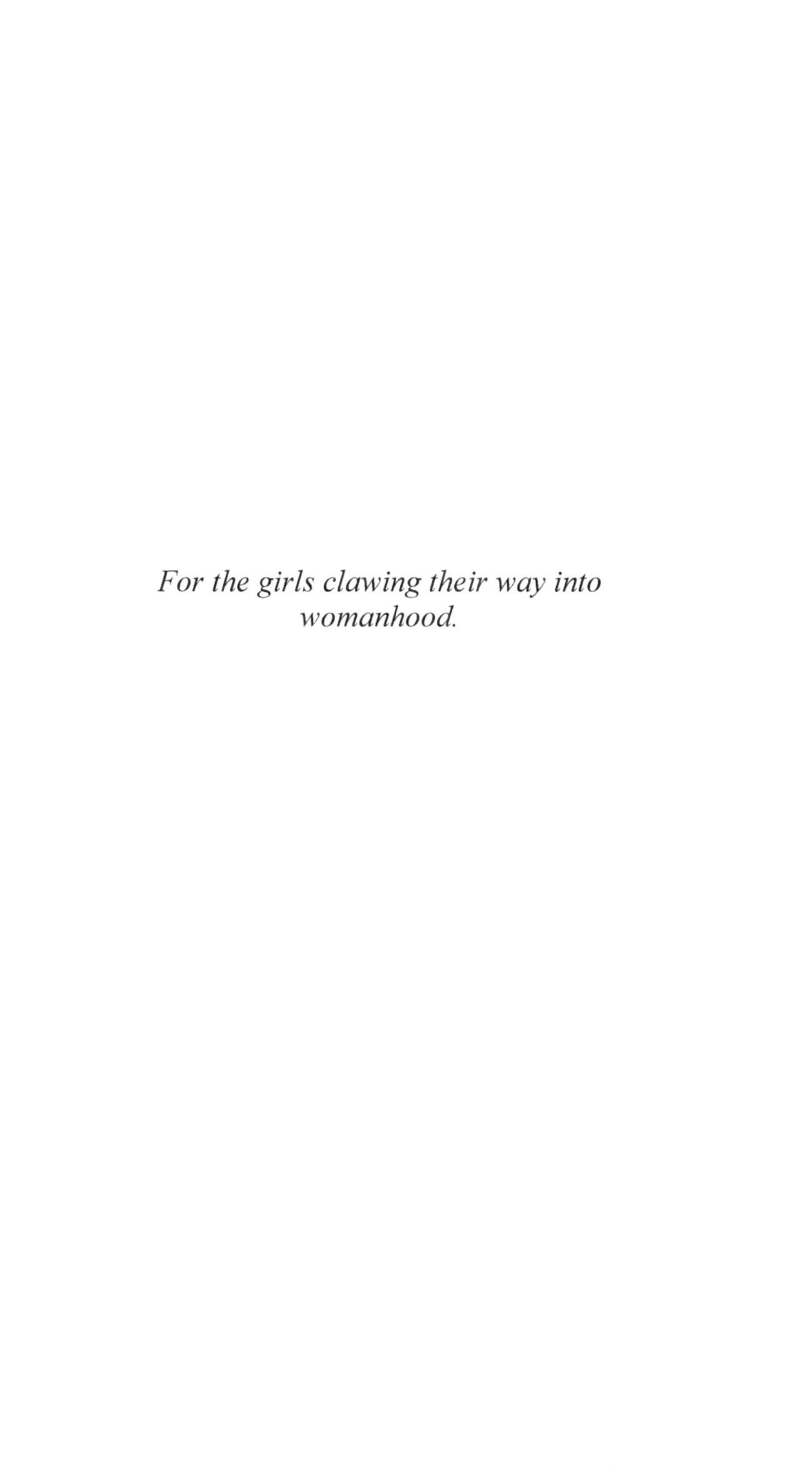

For the girls clawing their way into womanhood.

ACKNOWLEDGEMENT

Cheers to sobriety.

Warning: This Poem is not Meant to be Read, but Consumed

This poem is about food

and

Sex

and

Drugs

or:

all the things I would become addicted to if I
had time and money

You feed me in French

all this les poisson passion

I'm not biting

cause the last time I was on your hook

I thought I tasted gold

it was just the sour lemons

You were trying to spin me

and I've seen the girls you've got on your
spinning wheel these days

Rapunzel's blonde

lock-

ed

in a tower

I bet you look so radiant

climbing

down

her slender back

to basics:

I know she's spun you

all the good drugs

your bodies bending together on benzos

YOU'RE SO BLESSED

it's beautiful

how all these girls look like sheets

strung out to dry

Well we haven't spoken much

these days

so

you should know

I'm so high on how to be a lady

I keep spare

etiquette

in my back pocket

tell all the boys

raise your expectations as high as you want

I'll surpass them till they are cracks in the
motherfucking sidewalk

keep mine low in return

so you can step right on 'em

break a back

to basics

See

all this sex

is subtext:

it implies attraction

I remember when we were main

squeezing

the life

out of each other

I'd be making faces at you while you sleep

you couldn't discern from your snores

so it won't matter if this face

is frowning at you from a distance

paramount to a diameter

cause you were always sleeping so subtle

under covers where we

fornicated fore

you passed out from all the drugs

See

all this sex

is science

and you're just playing with my

chemistry

well that's the inevitability of desirability

beauty meets beast

and all my anecdotes become incidental

99% of my adult life has been lived in a
language I don't speak

tripping on

tongues

like they're transient

I take all the things you say in one ear

switch the pronouns

and it's out the other

under

oath

Intimacy is a vow that ends in

til death do us

PRIVATE

part (s)

of me

see

that as God's go

I translate to destruction

so I can't expect this feast to feed much more

then our egos

but

honey

I'm a sucker for the sweet things

saccharine sentiment

guess you could be the sprinkles on my Sunday

dinner

party

dress-

ed

to kill

it makes sense to dine and ditch

before dessert

when

gastronomically speaking

I'm gluttonous

for good loving

and a little

gateau

Still:

I'd like to keep my head in this matter

LET THEM

boys

EAT CAKE

Life by Numbers

3.

pregnancies

2 living

1 dead

2.

years old

our daughter was

when your girlfriend graduated from high school

1.

cancer scare

2 procedures

3 levels of dysplasia

0.

times I've been divorced

married

arrested

Hunting Season

I watched a grown man

shoot a bird

and then sob

because it couldn't fly

we sat in silence

the entire car

ride

home

I ask too manty questions

I tell too many tales

he said my name in the exhausted way

one speaks to a child

as if to say

not one

more

word

just

stop

I want to ask him things

I know

he'll never answer

are you scared?

because I am

even air

is

toxic

these days

I think we shared something

the moment

that bird fell from the sky

a kind of

mourning

for every action

we've taken

we're just killing ourselves

slowly

and now all at once

upon a time

I used to think I could make any man love me

so pluck my

feathers

until I'm bare

flesh

boned

and suck my marrow

until I'm dead ass

stoned

there's no cure for dying

it just takes one shot

there's a fear of flying

but that's all I've got

First Time

The first drug I ever did was heroin.

The rapper sat across from me. He was on the
phone. He motioned to me not to do it.

Fernie lit it.

He worked for Wells Fargo.

That was a nickname.

He was the same one

that carried me to the couch.

Passed out.

also anorexic.

When I went down

my very small

tits

were exposed

they could not call for help

but they were ready

for

sex

and he carried me to the couch

that man

that lit the fire

he saved me

and I wonder

to this day

if he is alive.

Vital Signs

At the doctor.

Blood Pressure: 95/63

Do you normally run low?

Lady,

I run so low

I run solo

Weight: 122

You've lost quite a bit of weight.

Lady,

I don't eat

unless it's my feelings

I don't eat

unless it's my words

Pulse: 77

Well, lady,

That was a good year

guess only my thoughts are racing

He trimmed the fat

said he's better off without me

Well, there's truth in that

Cause it's $169 for therapy

don't even get wined

or dined

It's three easy payments

of 19.99

to get to me

Don't have a warranty

just

return

policies

If I Were a Poet-Tree, I'd be a Weeping Willow

Sister said,

"You're nothing but a man-eater"

And I chewed on that

Long and hard

Cause diets

are a girl's best friend

and my secret to satiation is that

I'm always consuming

being eaten

alive.

Ingredients for how to start me simmering?

Shit,

I like grammar rules

And long division

So boy

put your

Eyes

Before

Ease

Except after

See

all

you're looking for is someone

To fill the intercostal voids

Where women were made from

RIBBED

meat

FOR YOUR PLEASURE

modern day romance

Is all but dead

So sorry to snitch

On this sad

situation

snatch

what's being sought

with a loosening of these laurels

while we debase our morals

Together

we're a train wreck

On a fast feeding frenzy

Combating alone time with

addictions

No, I never did depend on alcohol

But your attention

is 80 proof

Positive

That I'm better off

alone

I'm a woman

Of dark hair

Pale skin

colored

In the lines

So that puts me on the edge of VANITY

FAIR

To say if this were a string

I'd be dangling

on the precipice of your vowels

at the peak of your syllables

It's an I

And a U

And a sometimes

Why

Questions seems concerning to me

So I think I'll raise my voice

An octave above object

ification

hum these chords

through the phone cord

through the dime store

through the point where

what matters most is knowing

time is temporary

and I put a memory of you on my wrist

watch

the minutes tick into hours

these second hands sound silly

but for every sixty

I'm settling

My stomach

Ache

It was great

But I'm full on

Full frontal

and I'm French

so

j'ai faim

I.

Have .

Hunger.

For the human nature necessities

to

Eat

Drink

Man

Woman

It's the BOOK OF RITES

My right

To consume

And assume

You,

Sister,

Presumed

wrong

$$(L(p \times f) + C(t \times s)) - (P \times A)$$

Things I've lost:

my mind

my figure

that one

sock

Those

Miu Miu glasses

Well:

I gave good face

once

I focus on that damn sock:

lost in tangled bedsheets

like the thoughts

on my tripped

up tongue

Gone to the dryer

in heat

like myself:

We are both strung up

to dry

Every time I think I've

Found

the right words

I'm overextended on the metaphors:

I become a meta whore

Well:

Losing your life is a sure path to

Sainthood

Finding a penny's

A sure sign to do good

And lost socks sit silent

Wherever they go:

Warm heart

Cold feet

with nothing to show

Paper Trail

In my

30's

I have written

more

safety

plans

than

checks

warning signs:

this pulsing feeling

my feelings

are

eating

me

alive

so I

lie

say

someone else

will

dole

out

my pills

warning label reads:

may cause Stevens Johnson syndrome

if used

incorrectly

just what I need

another man

fucking up

my

heart

strings

and it probably

stings

if your skin turns red

and begins to

blister

an inside out

slow

burn

for a mind

on

fire

before you sign

as if to say

I solemnly swear

I'm

safe

inside

myself

they ask

for

three

people

you can call

in case of

emergency

like listing

your

job

references

if your only skill set

is

survival

it was always

you

I put

first

the only

phone number

I know

by

heart

attack

I left a symbolic

blank

line

and the doctor

still

signed

off

took the carbon copy

paper

tale

my file

getting

thicker

than my

thighs

I surmise

that someday

this will

end up

in

the shred

her

bits of confetti

in the

waste(d)

paper

basket

Waiting for the Recourse While I Consume Four Courses -or- In Which Gretchen and I go out for Lunch and Encounter a Mean Woman

Today I sat

head of the table

Lunching

on some conversation

par for the porridge

I was

goldilocksing

my motivation

to make mistakes

clockwise

or counter

cause I've never met a man

I couldn't convince myself

I loved

one feels too hot

one burns too cold

and this one is

just right

testing for the taste

smells like rose

bud

ing romance

til it's time to put the fork

down

ate my own words

now I

wait

for the recourse

cause love is best chewed

before swallowed

take it down deep

girl

cause it's gonna come out out

shit

on

second helpings

sloppy timing

for such a

sweet thing

well

you said a little heartbreak never hurt anyone

unless it was an attack

of the myocardial

degree

an infarction

infracted

from the social norms

your talk is cheap

and pretty girls

make the best

conversation

fodder for your

feature

broke in

bedded down

ate my way through the meal

til I was quickly your rumor

mill

ed

about

this milieu

put YOUR fork down

eat YOUR words

judge a girl by her cover

read her book backward

start with my last line

up

go

tit for

tattoo

cause lady, I'm just trying to dine

here

and you think you can shame me?

starved for attention

or binging on

bad feelings

you bit off more than you could chew

now give me this metaphor

so I can swallow it down

lick my lips

to taste

how sweet it is

Sac le Bleu

I haven't shaved since
the last time we had sex. Call
it my mourning bush.

Self Awareness

I'm such a

dumb

sad

bitch.

I mean

savage

Meditation on a Dead Bird

At the library

a thud

against the window

-the sound of a bird-

taking its dying

breath

Feathers

Flew

Furiously

as if to create

a funeral

shroud.

And

I looked

To see if

perhaps

the bird

had withstood

my witnessing

it's kamikazie

climb

toward the end of the earth

its wing fluttered

and it never

flew.

And

I wonder

how solemn a death

it must be

to hit a window

thinking to fly inside

display its grace

among the great

tomes

glass

never was

a barrier

even flight

could breach.

And

with its final breath

I wonder

what it felt

at the end of life

a final wing

rising

toward the unsuspecting wind.

And

aren't we all

relatives

of the great

age

when dinosaurs

became birds

and man

became beast?

And

aren't we all attempting

to fly toward freedom

with just that one barrier

masking a mirage

making a mess of things

when

prone to flight

we

instead

perish?

And

today

it was the birds

turn

to tumble

to try

the impossible

of coming from the outside

in.

And

if it had lived

would there have been a lesson

or is it so

that dead birds

create carrion

for the cat

that satisfaction

always brings

back?

Bitches, Ex's, and Ohhhs

I cat-called karma

well she's a bitch like me

played with all the boys like toys

I'm a barbie girl

with less career

opportunity

I'll draw my own conclusions

but can't color in the lines

he gave me his ex's stapler

I'm a sucker for good finds

know how it feels to be the last X

us girls who used to say O

passed down that plastic, pink torch

stapled to you

I still gotta

go

this karma will cut me

It comes back

like depression

you know I'd watch you

fuck her

like bitch,

you've learned your lesson

Falling Trees

I took nude photos

If I can't send them to you

am I pretty now?

My Baby Daddy's Baby Mama

Found out my baby daddy

has a baby

Well,

really a man,

now

Got offended offhand

I'm a farmer's market failure

thought only I had those

good eggs

But,

I can't complain about feelings

when I bought crotchless panties

to impress a married man

Then,

an attack of moral consciousness

showed me who I am

So,

He has a son

I have crotchless panties

And,

We're both reeling from

our acquisitions

Vaginas,

man.

They can be cold

You, Me, and STD's

I thought that I had herpes

It's so simple

It's so complex

Call it

Simplex

I've tried eating my feelings

I've tried drinking my feelings

I've found feeling my feelings

An exercise in failed fortitude

This time

I slid my feelings between my thighs

Let men make a molehill out of me

From a mountain of pain

And I poured it out

In fake orgasm

The kind you learn

When no touch

Feels right

So I'm gonna write it down

All the things I did

A shame spiral from a fountain pen

I'll splash the grief upon my own

Skin

Tattoo a scarlet letter

Walk around like I've got that red on my chest

Expect the best when I've exercised

All of the worst

Options

A woman could wonder at

Wander into

And I think that dating apps

Are really just a way

To play Candy Crush with your

Vagina

When you level up

The lines become so blurry

All the sweetness

Is just a stockpile

Of crossed lines

Blurred boundaries

And,

I do not have herpes.

Call it simple

Call it complex

I call it simplex

I Told Him This Poem is About Us

You,

the mortar

Me,

the pestle

I'll grind you down

until you're skin and

-bone

to pick with you

about all the stupid

shit I do

Trust me.

I don't trust me either.

Honey,

I want you to keep your distance

a little closer

Vicious cycle

like we're Sid and Nancy

you liked my grammar

oh she punctuates so sassy

Now I run on all my run on sentences

Borderline, baby

it's opposite day

and don't you like oppositional play?

No ring on my finger

yet we're still engaging

I wonder what battle

it is that we're waging

Well,

we're both bastards now.

There's no use complaining

Honey,

I want you to keep your distance

a little closer

Mind Fuck

I've upgraded

to

bi-weekly

therapy

sessions

one

just a quick

digital

drop

in

so much introspection

between me and my

sobriety

it's my

bestie

cause the only one I want to

see

this much

ugly

is

me

that's why I like addicts

get it

Get it?

sister said

only I could fuck my life up

this much

and have it work out

well, she's not wrong

I'm charming

as

been so guilty

been so innocent

that's why I'll never fix

it

my

chipped

tooth

just kidding

I can't

afford

that

cause

there's so much profit

from

this sickness

you know they got to keep us

thirsting

so girls

get your meds right

and girls

keep your

vag

tight

don't forget to

act

right

and retaliate:

ditch the

booze

cause we're so hook-line-and-sinker

generation of chronic

overthinkers

career goal

self

commodity

it's outrageous to

me

what a

mind fuck

it is to

be

alive

Little Children

72

my mother taught me how to starve
I see why I became this
resented that I trauma
so loudly
so proudly
there's a constant need
an honest greed
to be forgiven
my sins
mama taught me to starve
cause she was eaten
by sadness
we are all
just little
children
trying to outrun
our parents

Ego Drive-By

Ye said

baby I'm free

like a homeless person

felt that

right in

my

no less

soul

less

self

I'm a 37

year-

old

baby

took away my

security

blanket

in

sobriety

found out

my

soul

sought

object

permanence

was too busy

looking

for the next

high

an ego

drive

by

no chill just

all cry

a little something to

calm my nerves

to polish pearls

shucks.

cheers

to the fat

men

getting

good

off

addiction

in for a penny

chow down

on the pound

what's flesh anyway

but a thrift store

find

for the wine

and dimed

feel so dumb

these days

cause I've got no

bandwidth

I got no man

with

no

sandwich

to stuff

my

insecurities

ditched the prozac

calmed the noise

apps

drew a line down

new girl in

old

town

live less

stag-

nant

now

leaning in

somehow

I came clean

to my teenage

daydream

girl

I still mourn my

potential.

I'm too dehydrated

to be

this

thirsty

so I let

my

God

serve

me

and

yes

sobriety

saved me

each drink

a noose

you could

hang me

co-dependence

my

nursery

you know sometimes it's

hard to be

freeing myself

from

me

Babe

my children will always be
heirs
to
alcohol
I nursed a bottle
longer
than
my babies
to
my
breast
I could cry
for
those
days I
could
not
walk
the length of the zoo
with
my small
son's
hand
too underweight
from the

trauma
to
risk
a
small
step
and I could cry
for the
season
I spent
away
from
them
sobering up
a mother-child
under
my
own
mother's gentle
care
but
baby
it was
here
I learned
the grace
of
that
bond

and it was here
I grew
from
two
feet
tall
to
the highest
peak
when I took
my
last
drink
and I said
sayonara
to
that wounded
woman
of
woe
how I
have
swaddled
myself
inside
sobriety
taken
care
to

nurture
each nighttime
with
storybook
voice
a brave
performance
no longer
an
act
fore
I am
your
mother
child
and darling
we
can
do
hard
things

www.ingramcontent.com/pod-product-compliance
Lightning Source LLC
LaVergne TN
LVHW011042200726
843509LV00011B/1331